TOP CHRISTIAN HITS OF '04-'05

ISBN 0-634-09553-6

HAL•LEONARD®
CORPORATION

7777 W. BLUEMOUND RD. P.O. BOX 13819 MILWAUKEE, WI 53213

Visit Hal Leonard Online at
www.halleonard.com

ALL

Words and Music by IAN ESKELIN,
BRIAN WHITE and TEDD TJORNHOM

I've had a world of pos - si - bil - i - ties

ALL I NEED

Words and Music by BETHANY DILLON,
ED CASH and DAVE BARNES

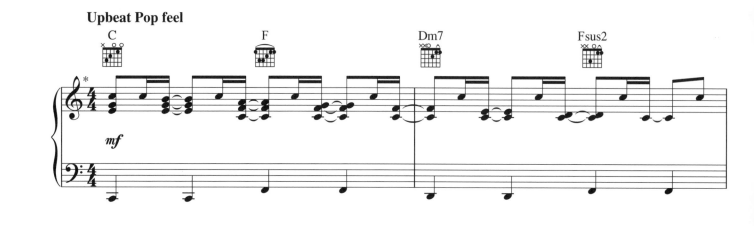

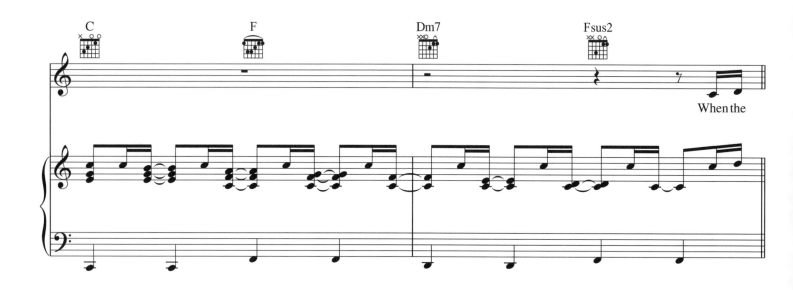

When the

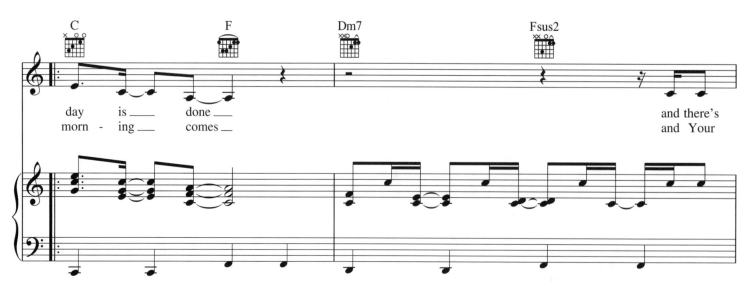

day is ___ done ___
morn - ing ___ comes ___

and there's
and Your

Recorded a half step lower.

You fill me _____ when _ I'm emp -

- ty. There is noth - ing else; ___ You're __ all I ___ need. __

When the

You fill me ____ when ___ I'm emp - ty. There is noth - ing else; ___ You're ___ all I ____ need, ___ You're ___ all I ____ need. ___

ALL THINGS NEW

Words and Music by
STEVEN CURTIS CHAPMAN

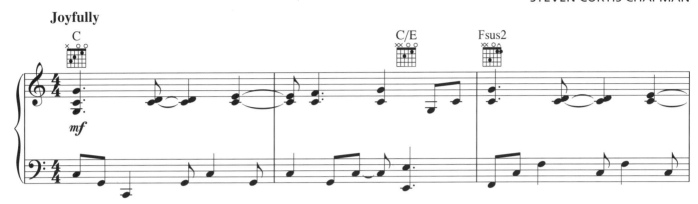

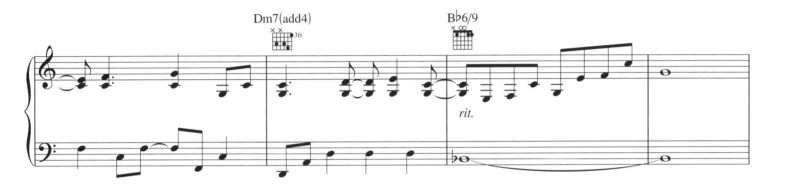

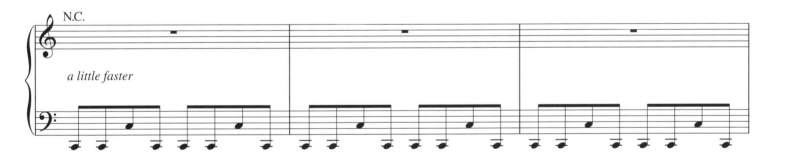

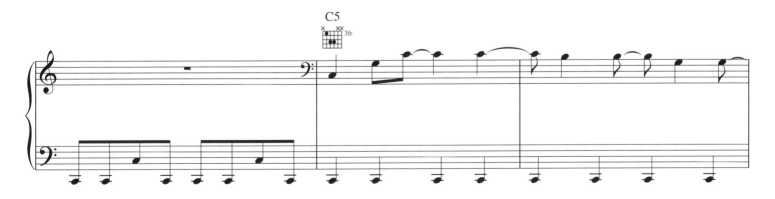

BEAUTIFUL

Words and Music by BETHANY DILLON
and ED CASH

Brightly, in one

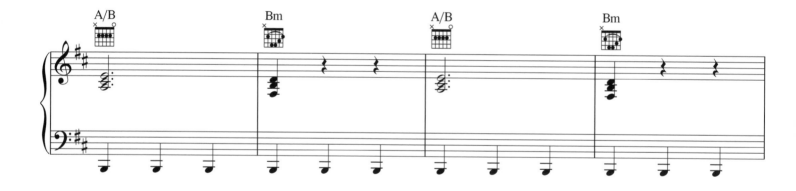

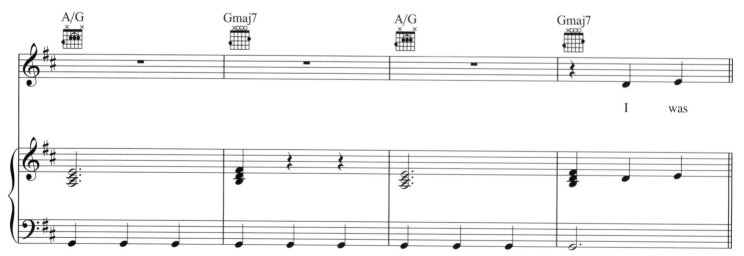

I was

Recorded a half step lower.

Beau - ti - ful. _____

(Vocal 1st time only)

Repeat and Fade

Optional Ending

BEAUTIFUL NAME

Words and Music by LYNN NICHOLS,
TEDD TJORNHOM, CHRISSY CONWAY,
ALISA GIRARD and KRISTIN SWINFORD

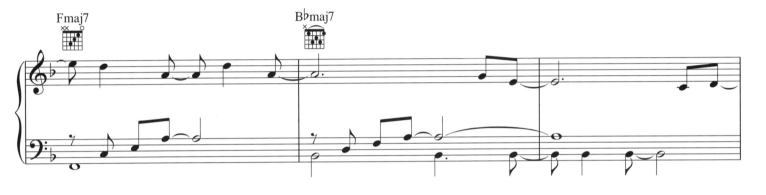

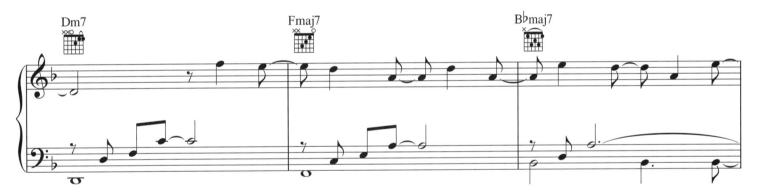

Your heart I seek ___ to find. ___
Should all life cease ___ to grow, ___

D.S. al Coda

new pace. I ____ know what my life is ____ for. ____ I ____ will run, ____

Em7

CODA

B♭sus2   F5   D5

____ Your beau - ti - ful Name. _____

Instrumental solo

B♭sus2   F5   C5   C5/A   D5

Your beau - ti - ful Name. __

B♭sus2   F5

BLESSED BE YOUR NAME

Words and Music by MATT REDMAN
and BETH REDMAN

*Recorded a half step lower.

FILLED WITH YOUR GLORY

Words and Music by TIM NEUFELD
and JON NEUFELD

Yeah.

COME ON BACK TO ME

Words by MAC POWELL
Music by TAI ANDERSON, BRAD AVERY,
DAVID CARR, MARK LEE and MAC POWELL

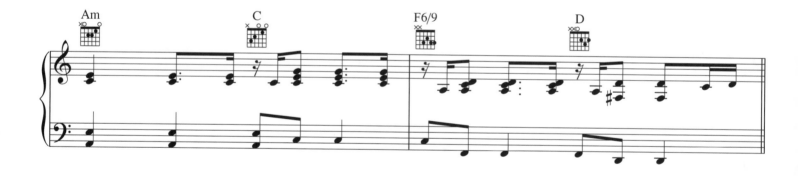

Well, you've been hid - ing now __ for so __ long

GRAVITY

Words and Music by SHAWN McDONALD
and CHRIS STEVENS

The ways of this world are grab-bing a-
This world keeps mak-ing me cry, but I'm

hold. Won't let me go, won't let me fly by.
gon-na try, gon-na try to fly, gon-na fly high.

It's tak-ing its toll down on my soul,
Don't wan-na give in to the sin,

'cause I know what I need in my life. ___ Don't let ___ me ___ lose ___
wan-na stay in You till the end. ___ Don't want ___ to ___ lose

I don't wan - na fall ____ a - way __ from You. __

Grav - i - ty is pull - ing me __ to the ground. __

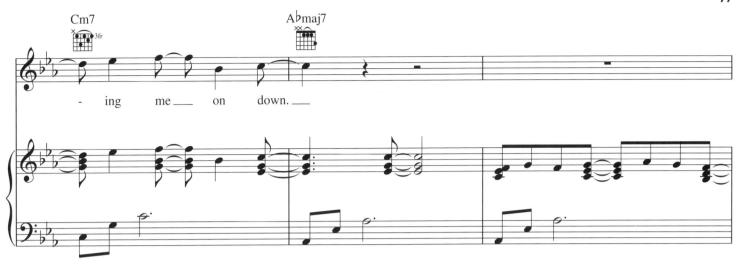

-ing me ___ on down. ___

I don't wan - na fall ___ a - way ___ from You. ___

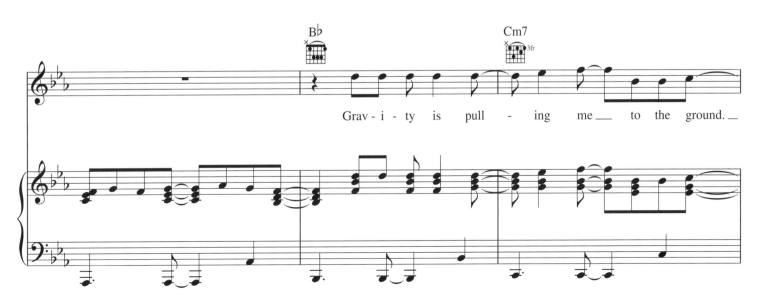

Grav - i - ty is pull ___ ing me ___ to the ground. ___

HEALING RAIN

Words and Music by MATT BRONLEEWE,
MICHAEL W. SMITH and MARTIN SMITH

Steady four

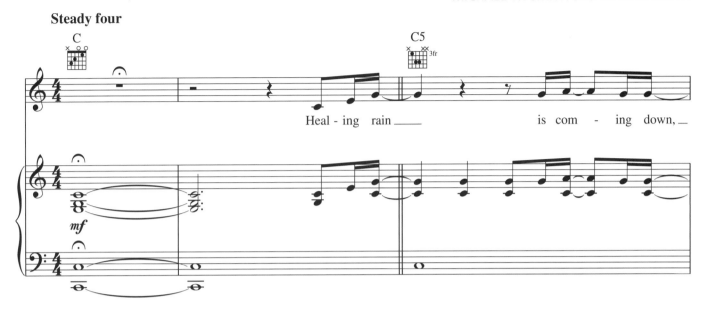

Heal - ing rain ___ is com - ing down, ___

it's com - ing near - er ___ to this old town. ___

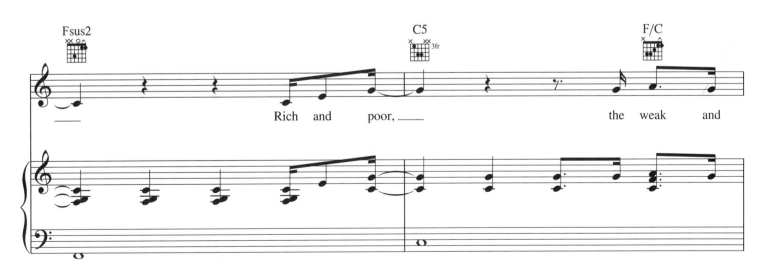

Rich and poor, ___ the weak and

*Recorded 1/2 step higher

HE IS EXALTED

Words and Music by
TWILA PARIS

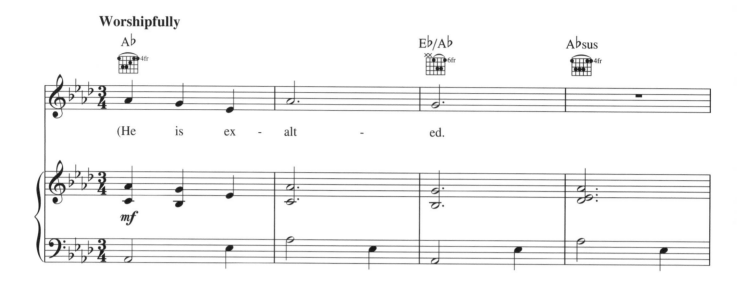

Worshipfully

(He is ex- alt- ed.

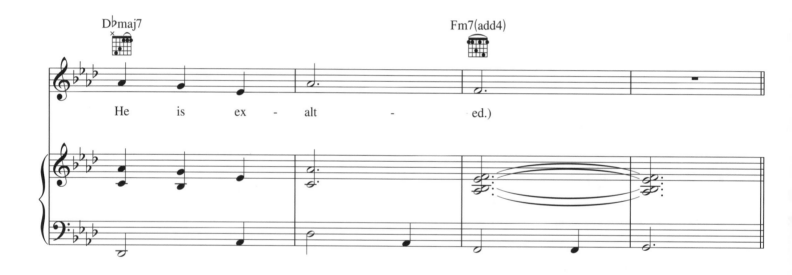

He is ex- alt- ed.)

He is ex- alt- ed, the King is ex- alt- ed on

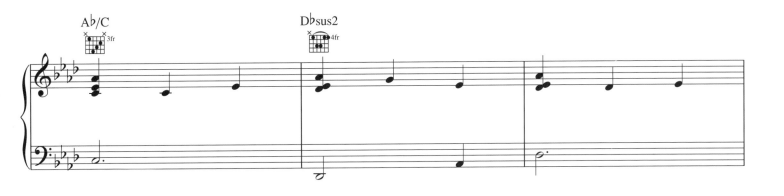

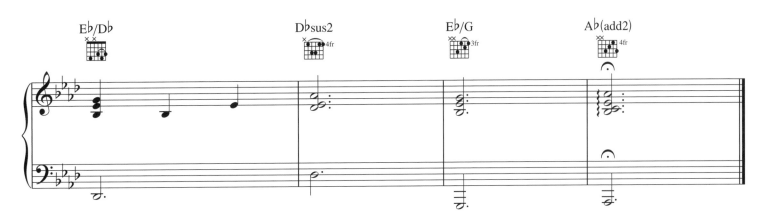

HERE WITH ME

Words and Music by BRAD RUSSELL,
BART MILLARD, MICHAEL SCHEUCHZER, JAMES BRYSON,
ROBIN SHAFFER, NATHAN COCHRAN, BARRY GRAUL,
DAN MUCKALA and PETER KIPLEY

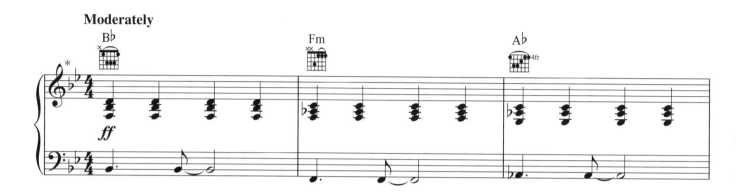

I long for Your em - brace

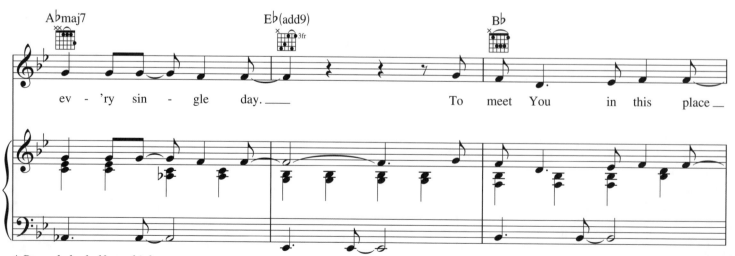

ev - 'ry sin - gle day. ___ To meet You in this place ___

Recorded a half step higher.

MORE

Words and Music by KENNY GREENBERG,
JASON HOUSER and MATTHEW WEST

Take a look at the moun-tain stretch-ing a mile____ high. Take a look at the o-cean, far as your eye can____ see,____ and

I BELIEVE

Words by MAC POWELL
Music by TAI ANDERSON, BRAD AVERY,
DAVID CARR, MARK LEE and MAC POWELL

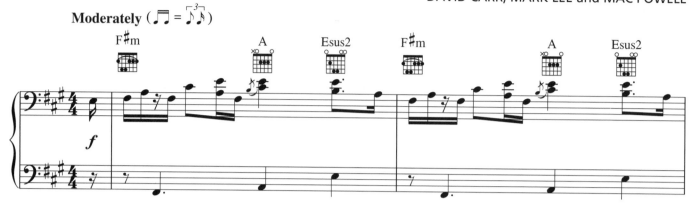

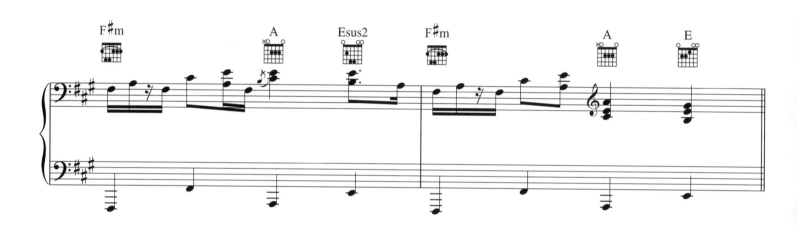

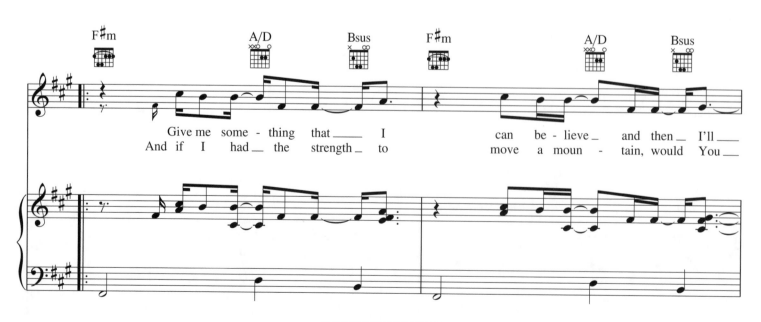

Give me some-thing that ___ I can be-lieve ___ and then ___ I'll ___
And if I had ___ the strength ___ to move a moun - tain, would You ___

114

IF WE ARE THE BODY

Words and Music by
MARK HALL

MUCH OF YOU

Words and Music by
STEVEN CURTIS CHAPMAN

YOU ARE GOD ALONE
(not a god)

Words and Music by BILLY J. FOOTE
and CINDY FOOTE

*Recorded a half step lower.

un - stop - pa - ble, ___ that's what You are. ___

RIGHT HERE

Words and Music by
JEREMY CAMP

All the world ___ is watch - ing;
All these thoughts ___ I've wast - ed,

all the world ___ does care. ___
all these thoughts ___ I've feared. ___

VOICE OF TRUTH

Words and Music by MARK HALL
and STEVEN CURTIS CHAPMAN

WALK BY FAITH

Words and Music by
JEREMY CAMP

Slowly, steadily in 1

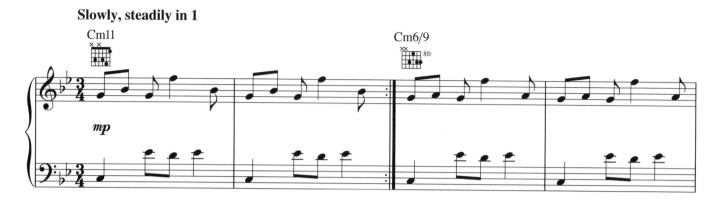

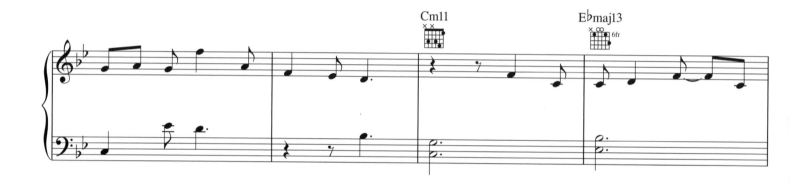

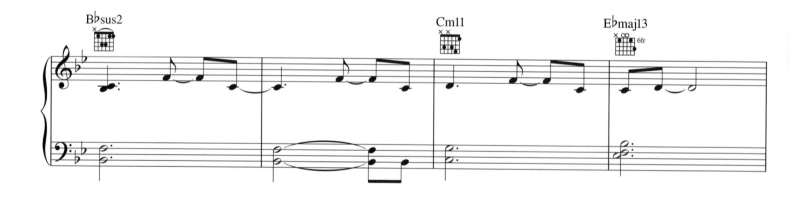

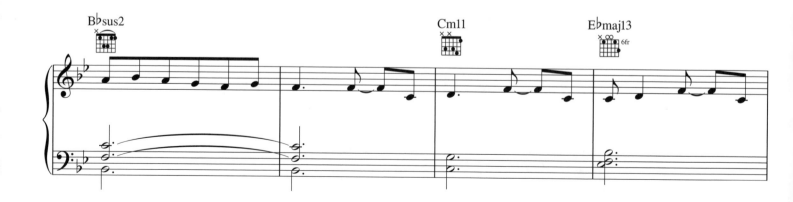

WHO AM I

Words and Music by
MARK HALL

YOU WERE THERE

Words and Music by
BEN GLOVER

Melody is written one octave higher than sung
Original key: E♭ major. This edition has been transposed down one half-step to be more playable.